GERMANY

A TRUE BOOK®

by
Susan H. Gray

Children's Press®

A Division of Scholastic Inc.

New York Toronto London Auckland Sydney
Mexico City New Delhi Hong Kong
Danbury, Connecticut

Romerberg, Frankfurt, Germany

Content Consultant
Professor Kit Belgum
*Department of
Germanic Studies
University of Texas
at Austin*

Reading Consultant
Nanci R. Vargus, Ed.D.
*Assistant Professor
Literacy Education
University of Indianapolis
Indianapolis, IN*

*The photograph on the
cover shows the
Neuschwanstein Castle in
Bavaria. The photograph on
the title page shows flags
along a river in Hamburg.*

Library of Congress Cataloging-in-Publication Data

Gray, Susan H.
    Germany / by Susan H. Gray.
        p. cm. — (A true book)
    Summary: Presents information on the geography, history, people,
economy, and social life and customs of Germany, one of the largest
countries in Europe.
    Includes bibliographical references and index.
    ISBN 0-516-22673-8 (lib. bdg.) 0-516-27753-7 (pbk.)
    1. Germany—Juvenile literature. 2. Germany—History—Juvenile
literature . 3. Germany—Social life and customs—Juvenile literature
[1. Germany.] I. Title. II. Series.
DD17 .G713 2003
943—dc21   2001008490

CHILDREN'S PRESS, AND A TRUE BOOK®, and associated logos are
trademarks and or registered trademarks of Grolier Publishing Co., Inc.
SCHOLASTIC and associated logos are trademarks and or registered
trademarks of Scholastic Inc.

1 2 3 4 5 6 7 8 9 10 R 12 11 10 09 08 07 06 05 04 03

Contents

Mountains, Rivers, Forests, and Plains

Germany is one of the largest countries in Europe. It borders nine other countries and two seas. With 137,821 square miles (356,955 square kilometers), it is a little smaller than the state of Montana. About 82 million people live in Germany. This is more than one-fourth the number of people living in the whole United States!

Germany is divided up into sixteen states. Each state has its own capital. Berlin is the largest city in the country. Berlin is also a state and the capital of the whole country. Other major cities include Hamburg, Munich, Cologne, Frankfurt, and Stuttgart.

Much of northern Germany is a large, flat area, or plain.

Many farms are located in the northern part of the country.

Some of the country's richest farmlands lie in this region. Central Germany is made up of tree-covered mountains and river valleys. This area is home to deer, wild pigs, and foxes.

7

The Alps extend through southern Germany.

Southern Germany has the highest mountains in the country. A European mountain range called the Alps reaches into southern Germany. The highest point in the country is on Zugspitze, an Alpine mountain rising 9,721 feet (2,963 meters).

The Black Forest is in southwest Germany. The forest is known for its dark fir trees, fresh springs, and fine hiking trails. Several small rivers come together in the Black Forest. They form the Danube, which is the second-longest river in Europe. The Danube flows

The beautiful Danube River flows through Bavaria.

east for almost 1,800 miles (2,900 km) and empties into the Black Sea. Its beautiful scenery has inspired artists and musicians for hundreds of years. Another river, the

Elbe, flows from the Czech Republic and empties near the busy German seaport of Hamburg near the North Sea.

The Rhine River is one of the busiest rivers in the world. Ships loaded with factory goods run up and down the river, which empties into the North Sea. Over the centuries, many cities have grown up along the Rhine. In more recent times, pollution has damaged the river.

Germany's People

Most of the country's people have grown up in Germany. However, about nine percent of the country's current population is originally from another country. Most of these foreigners are Turkish. For more than forty years, people from Turkey have

German children are dressed up in local costumes (above). Turkish workers are harvesting grapes in a German winery (right).

come to Germany to work. Many stay and raise their families.

Other foreigners have come from countries in eastern and

southern Europe. Some have come to escape harsh rulers in their own countries. Others have come to find jobs and to live in the cities.

Most of Germany's people live in cities. Berlin, Hamburg, and Munich have more than a million people each. Several other cities each have at least a half million people. Very few Germans live in the countryside.

About one-third of all Germans are Protestant. Most of them are Lutherans. Another

one-third are Roman Catholic. The rest belong to Jewish, Muslim, Hindu, or other faiths, or are not involved in religious practice.

Emperors, Kings, and Dukes

More than a thousand years ago, much of Europe was called the Holy Roman Empire. Charlemagne ruled it from the year 800 until his death in 814. The area we now know as Germany was part of this empire.

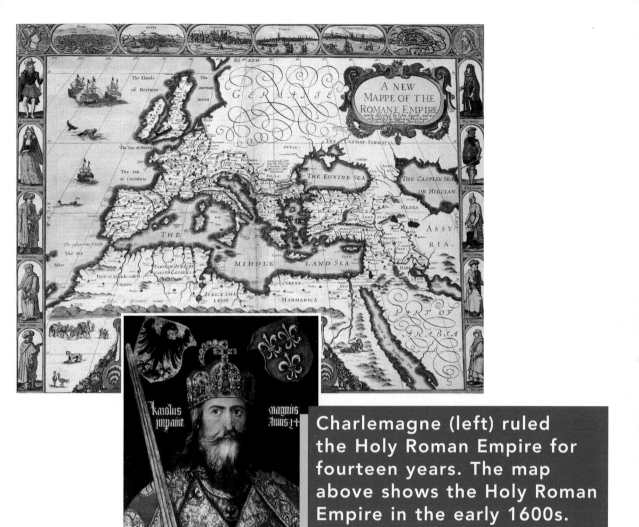

Charlemagne (left) ruled the Holy Roman Empire for fourteen years. The map above shows the Holy Roman Empire in the early 1600s.

For hundreds of years, the Holy Roman Empire withstood invaders and wars. Often, its

own rulers fought among them-
selves. The constant wars and
fighting made the empire grow
weak. Meanwhile, different rulers
were gaining power over small
parts of Germany. Many kings,
princes, and dukes were control-
ling their own little states. The
large state of Prussia was ruled
by King Wilhelm I, with Otto von
Bismarck as his prime minister.

Von Bismarck wanted Germany
to be united. He wanted to see it
grow strong. He joined many of
the small German states together.

Otto von Bismarck helped to unite several of the smaller German states.

By 1871, there was one nation of Germany. Wilhelm I became its emperor.

Then the states began to build up their **economies**. Factories started to spring up.

Steam trains moved goods and people through Germany in the 1800s.

New roads were built to connect growing cities. Powerful trains were rushing across the land on shiny new tracks. The united nation was indeed growing strong.

The Three B's

German history includes some musical **geniuses**. **Johann Sebastian Bach (1685–1750)** was a master musician and **composer**. His works are still heard today in churches and concert halls all over the world.

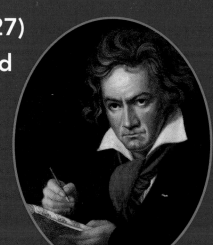

Johann Sebastian Bach

Ludwig van Beethoven (1770–1827) composed for piano and other instruments. Even after he became deaf, he still wrote magnificent works.

Ludwig van Beethoven

Johannes Brahms

Johannes Brahms (1833–1897) wrote pieces for piano, violins, singers, and orchestras. Bach, Beethoven, and Brahms are known as the "Three Bs."

Two Wars and a Wall

Wilhelm II became the next ruler of Germany. At the time, many countries were not getting along with one another. Across Europe, groups of people felt strongly united by the language, culture, and religion of their own countries. At the same time, European countries were each building up

Wilhem II was the emperor of Germany when World War I began.

their own armies and navies. Tensions grew and countries began to take sides with one another, in case war broke out. In 1914, Archduke Francis Ferdinand, an Austrian, was shot and killed by a man from Serbia. Within weeks, all of Europe plunged into what became World War I.

The war was a disaster for Germany. By the time it ended in 1918, more than six million Germans had lost their lives. The countries that won the war forced Germany to pay them gold and other goods. Germany also lost some of its territories after the war. Many Germans had bitter feelings about the losses.

After World War I, the country had many problems. People could not find jobs. The prices of food and clothes were very

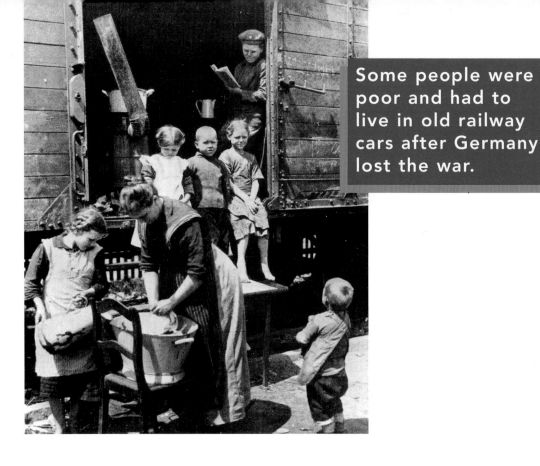

Some people were poor and had to live in old railway cars after Germany lost the war.

high. People began looking for a strong leader to save the country. For some, Adolf Hitler seemed to be the right man.

In 1933, Hitler became **chancellor** of Germany. He was

Adolf Hitler's harsh leadership and brutal acts led to World War II.

a ruthless man. He killed anyone who threatened his power. He also tried to kill off all the people he believed were **inferior**. He killed thousands of handicapped people and more than six million Jews. His brutal efforts to take over other countries led to World

War II. After six long years (1939–1945), the war ended. Germany had lost again.

After the war, the nation was divided into East and West Germany. The capital city of Berlin was also divided into east and west. West Germany and West Berlin were free to choose their own leaders. East Germany and East Berlin were led by a **communist** government. In 1961, the communists built a huge concrete wall in Berlin to separate east from west.

The Berlin Wall separated East and West Germany.

People in Berlin hated the wall. By 1989, the East Germans began protesting against their government. Their voices became so strong that finally one night the government opened the wall. One year later, Berlin was a united city and Germany was again a united nation.

The Wall Came Tumblin' Down

"Everyone's gone crazy!" The man was shouting at the top of his lungs. He could not believe his eyes. People were dancing on top of the Berlin Wall. Some people had hammers and were knocking chunks out of it. Thousands of people were streaming over it. For twenty-eight years, people from one side of Berlin could not visit the other side. Now everyone was going back and forth freely. People were crying for joy. Strangers were hugging one another. The wall had been a symbol of the divided Germany. When it came down, people rejoiced for months.

Germans break down the wall.

A piece of the old wall.

Germans at Work

Most people in Germany live in apartments. From home, they can often walk to school or to their neighborhood stores. School days are shorter than in the United States. German stores are usually smaller than U.S. stores, but large department stores and

A car moves down the production line at an automotive plant.

discount stores are becoming more popular in the country.

German factories are known for their fine products. Cars, planes, cameras, machines, and electronics from Germany are valued all over the world. Many factories are located in the west, along the Ruhr River. This area also produces much steel and iron.

Germany is also famous for its handmade items. Skilled wood carvers create toys and fine furniture. Other experts make glassware, crystal items, jewelry, and other fine products.

About one person in sixty works on a farm. Some farmers

Some Germans work on farms and grow fruits and vegetables.

raise pigs and cattle. Some grow wheat, potatoes, beets, apples, and other foods. They also grow vines called *hops*. Part of the hop plant is used in making beer. Germany is one of the biggest producers of hops in the world.

Forests cover about one-third of the country. Many forests have not been developed so people can enjoy camping and hiking there. Other forests provide work for people in the timber **industry**. Much of the wood is used in building houses. Some of the wood is also used to make cuckoo clocks.

Some people near the North and Baltic seas make their living by fishing. This can often be a dangerous job. Fishermen have

A clockmaker carves a wooden face for a cuckoo clock in his Black Forest workshop.

to face wild storms and icy waters. On good trips, they catch herring, cod, and flatfish. Also in the north, the important harbor city of Hamburg receives products from all over the world. Many people there work in the shipping industry.

Germans at Play

German children and grown-ups enjoy soccer and bicycle riding. They also like to hike and ski in the mountains. People come from all over the world to ski or go climbing in the Alps.

German families often take vacations to see other parts of the country. Sometimes they

Hiking in the mountains is a popular pastime in Germany.

drive on high-speed freeways. These are called *autobahns*. Sometimes they take one of the high-speed trains to cities in Germany or other countries in Europe.

Some people like a slower pace. They travel along a road called the Fairy Tale Route. It is a 400-mile (644-km) trip from Hanau to Bremen. In the 1800s, Jakob and Wilhelm Grimm traveled this area. They listened to people tell fairy

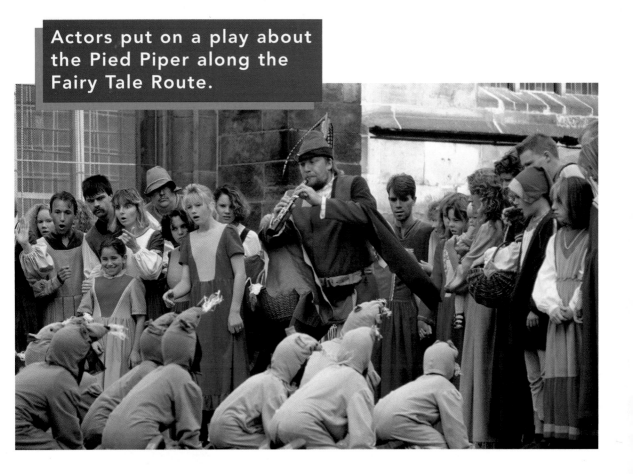

tales. The Brothers Grimm then printed books of the tales. Readers were **spellbound** by stories such as Cinderella, Hansel and Gretel, and Snow White.

Fresh sausage is on display at a butcher shop in Hamburg.

Some of Germany's favorite dishes are known all over the world. Such foods include sauerkraut, apple strudel, sausage, and potato dumplings. Germans are also famous for making beer and wine.

People especially enjoy the beer during Oktoberfest. This festival takes place in Munich every year in September and October. It started almost 200 years ago as a wedding feast in the state of Bavaria. The king of Bavaria was

A large crowd celebrates Oktoberfest in Munich.

getting married and he planned a big party. People celebrated all over town. Everyone had so much fun they decided to do it every year. Now, people come from all over the world for this great festival.

Visitors also come to see Germany's beautiful towns and countryside. Near the Baltic Sea, they relax on pretty, white beaches. In Cologne, they walk through Germany's most famous and **ornate** cathedral. In Passau, they listen to the largest pipe organ in Europe.

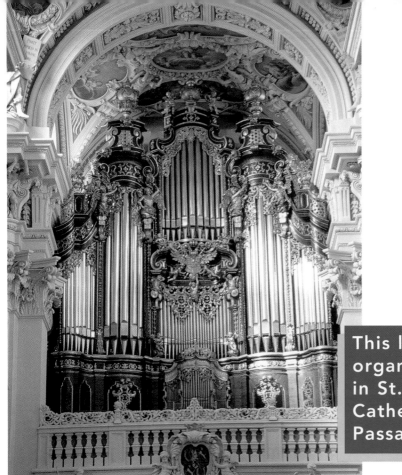

This large church organ is located in St. Stephen's Cathedral in Passau, Germany.

In the Alps, they tour the awesome castle built by King Ludwig II.

Germans are proud of their beautiful country and the many fine things they have given the world.

To Find Out More

Here are some additional resources to help you learn more about Germany:

Books

Davis, Kevin. **Look What Came From Germany.** Danbury, CT: Franklin Watts, 1999.

Knorr, Rosanne. **If I Lived in Germany**. New York: Longstreet Press, 1995.

Tunnell, Michael O. **Brothers in Valor: A Story of Resistance.** New York: Holiday House, 2001.

Venezia, Mike. **Johann Sebastian Bach.** Danbury, CT: Children's Press, 1998.

Organizations and Online Sites

German Embassy
4645 Reservoir Road
Washington, DC 20007-1998

German American National Congress (DANK)
4740 N. Western Avenue
Chicago, IL 60625-2097
The largest organization of Americans with German ancestry.

The German Embassy
http://www.germany-info.org

The German embassy's information center that covers travel, culture, government, business and more.

The Brothers Grimm
http://www-2.cs.cmu.edu/ ~spok/grimmtmp

A great site with links to more than 200 fairy tales collected by the Brothers Grimm.

German Castles
http://www.allgaeu-schwaben. com/castlemap.html

Photographs, histories, and tourist information on Germany's castles, including the ones in ruins.

Important Words

chancellor a high state official

communism a system where the government owns everything

composer someone who writes music

economy a country's wealth, based on its goods and services

genius a very smart or creative person

industry the making and selling of goods and services

inferior situated lower down

spellbound fascinated

Index

Meet the Author

Susan H. Gray has B.S. and M.S. degrees in zoology. She has worked as a writer for more than twenty-five years, producing many articles on science and medicine. She has also written a number of successful grant proposals for medical programs. However, she especially enjoys writing for younger audiences, and has written several books on scientific topics for children.

Susan lives in Cabot, Arkansas, with her husband Michael. She enjoys gardening and playing the piano.